OUR SOLAR SYSTEM- PLANETS AND EXOPLANETS VOLUME-1.1

VINIT YADAV

This book is dedicated to respected Astronomer **Anil Kumar Das.** Most of his scientific contributions were in the field of solar physics mainly as an experimenter in the spectrophotometric study of sunspots and the chromosphere. He contributed significantly to the development of the equipment present at the Kodaikanal Observatory and to the growth of numerous young researchers.

Contents

Author

The Author of this book- Our Solar system- Planets and exoplanets are Vinit Yadav. Born in a lower-middle-class family in a small village of Haryana. He is 15 years old while writing this book for astronomy lovers. He always wanted to share his knowledge of Astronomy with others.

This is his first book written towards Astronomy, and his second in life. And will share more knowledge with others through his books!

Hope you will get to learn something knowledgeable in this book.

Preface

Abstract

In this Volume-1.1, It is the research and its data carried out about the Birth of our Solar System, How it was formed (In brief). Formation of Planets- Solar Nebula theory, The gravitation of collapse, Condensation Of Solid, The Formation of Planetesimals to the formation of protoplanets and Growth of Protoplanet.

Further, it is about Planets present in our solar system (Two kinds of planets)- Terrestrial and Jovian Planets, Data related to them and their structure.

In this Volume 1.1, we will discuss terrestrial Planets (Their Atmosphere, Structure, and detailed data info)

Introduction

BIRTH OF THE SOLAR SYSTEM

created out of gas and dust, the sun first shone as a star within a ring of debris—the leftovers from its formation. these materials slowly grew from tiny particles into asteroids, moons, and planets.

Five billion years ago, the solar system did not exist. Our galaxy, the Milky Way, was already 8 billion years old, and within it, generations of stars had lived and died, seeding space with gas and dust that assembled into huge, dark clouds. Then, on the outskirts of the galaxy, something started to stir. An exploding star—a supernova—squeezed a neighboring dark cloud, which then began to collapse under its own gravity. Deep within, denser clumps of gas started to coagulate into thousands of protostars. As each one of these shrank, they heated up until nuclear reactions began in their cores, and stars were born. Many of these newly hatched stars were surrounded by whirling disks of gas and icy dust. In one case in particular—the newborn Sun—we know that this material, over millions of years, created the planets of our solar system.

Solar system nursery

Sheltered from the dangerous radiation of space, the new solar system developed in the depths of a giant bank of interstellar smog. This cloud was composed mainly of hydrogen and helium gas left over from the Big Bang and polluted with specks of soot and cosmic dust ejected from dying stars. It was so cold that gases such as methane, ammonia, and water vapor froze onto the tiny dust particles. These microscopic hailstones, whirling around the young Sun, were the seeds from which the planets would eventually grow.

99.8 percent of the Solar System's mass is found in the Sun.

Mystic Mountain Stars and planetary systems are being born today, in giant interstellar clouds like the stunning Mystic Mountain in the Carina Nebula. The protostars are hidden in the murk; but the outflowing jets from a young planetary system have blasted through as a pair of "horns" 2 trillion km (1.2 trillion miles) long.

Sun's secret birth Hidden in a nebula rich with chemical compounds, known as a molecular cloud, the embryonic Sun was no more than a collapsing clump of gas. As it contracted, this clump heated up to become a protostar.

Bipolar outflow The protostar began to rotate, generating a strong magnetic field that forced streamers of gas away in opposite directions. The gas collapsing around the protostar turned ever faster and flattened out.

Lighting up The protostar grew hot enough to ignite nuclear reactions, and the Sun began to shine. Its heat boiled away the ice nearby, leaving only rocky dust in the inner disk. But icy grains still survived on the outer edges.

Space rubble The rubble left over from the building of the solar system still falls to Earth as meteorites. The rare stony meteorites known as carbonaceous chondrites have remained unchanged since the birth of the planets. By analyzing the radioactive atoms in them, scientists can pinpoint the exact age of the solar system: 4.5682 billion years old. The oldest meteorites contain chondrules, glassy drops of melted rock formed in the heat generated by the development of the **solar system.**

1

Formation Of Planets

The story of Planet Formation

The challenge for modern planetary scientists is to compare the observed characteristics of the solar system with predictions of the solar nebula theory, so they can work out details of how the planets formed.

The Chemical Composition of the Solar Nebula

The solar nebula would have had the same composition as interstellar gas clouds. Such clouds are mostly hydrogen with some helium and small amounts of the heavier elements.

That is precisely what you see in the composition of the sun. Analysis of the solar spectrum shows that the sun is mostly hydrogen, with a quarter of its mass being helium and only about 2 percent being heavier elements. This must have been the composition of the solar nebula, and you can also see that composition reflected in the chemical compositions of the planets. The small inner planets are composed of rock and metal, and the large outer planets are rich in low-density gases such as hydrogen and helium. The chemical

composition of Jupiter resembles the composition of the sun. Furthermore, if you allowed low-density gases to escape from a blob of stuff with the same overall composition as the sun or Jupiter, the relative proportions of the remaining heavier elements would resemble Earth's chemical composition.

The Condensation of Solids

An important clue to understanding the process that converted the nebular gas into solid matter is the variation in density among solar system objects. You have already noted that the four inner planets are small and have high density, resembling Earth, whereas the outermost planets are large and have low density, resembling Jupiter.

Even among the four Terrestrial planets, you will find a pattern of slight differences in density. Merely listing the observed densities of the Terrestrial planets does not reveal the pattern clearly because Earth and Venus, being more massive, have stronger gravity and have squeezed their interiors to higher densities. The uncompressed densities — the densities the planets would have if their gravity did not compress them, or, to put it another way, the average densities of their original construction materials — can be calculated using the actual densities and masses of each planet.

In general, the closer a planet is to the sun, the higher its uncompressed density

This density variation originated when the solar system first formed solid grains. The kind of matter that could condense in a particular region depended on the temperature of the gas there. In the inner regions, the temperature of condensation was evidently 1500 K or so. The only materials that can form grains at that temperature are compounds with high melting points, such as metal oxides and pure metals, which are very dense. Farther out in the nebula it was cooler, and silicates (rocky material) could also condense, in addition to metal. These are less dense than metal oxides and metals. Mercury, Venus, Earth, and Mars are evidently composed of a mixture of metals, metal oxides, and silicates, with proportionately more metals closer to the sun and more silicates.

Observed and Uncompressed Densities

Farther from the sun. Even farther from the sun there was a boundary called the ice line beyond which water vapor could freeze to form ice particles. Yet a little farther from the sun, compounds such as methane and ammonia could condense to form other types of ice. Water vapor, methane, and ammonia were abundant in the solar nebula, so beyond the ice line the nebula would have been filled with a blizzard of ice particles, mixed with small amounts of silicate and metal particles that could also condense there. Those ices are low-density materials. The compositions of Jupiter and the other outer planets include a mix of ices plus relatively small amounts of silicates and metal.

The sequence in which the different materials condense from the gas as you move away from the sun toward lower temperature is called the **condensation sequence**. It suggests that the planets, forming at different distances from the

The Condensation Sequence

sun, should have accumulated from different kinds of materials in a predictable way. People who have read a little bit about the origin of the solar system may hold the Common Misconception that the matter in the solar nebula was sorted by density, with the heavy rock and metal sinking toward the sun and the low-density gases being blown outward. That is not the case. The chemical composition of the solar nebula was originally approximately the same throughout the disk. The important factor was temperature: The inner nebula was hot, and only metals and rock could condense there, whereas the cold outer nebula could form lots of ices along with metals and rock. The ice line seems to have been between Mars and Jupiter, and it separates the region for formation of the high-density Terrestrial planets from that of the low-density Jovian planets.

The Formation of Planetesimals

In the development of a planet, two processes operate to collect solid bits of matter — rock, metal, ice — into larger bodies called planetesimals, which eventually build the planets. The study of planetesimal building is the study of these processes: condensation and accretion, each of which will be described in detail in this section.

According to the solar nebula theory, planetary development in the solar nebula began with the growth of dust grains. These specks of matter, whatever their composition, grew from microscopic size first by condensation, then by accretion.

A particle grows by condensation when it adds matter one atom or molecule at a time from a surrounding gas. Snowflakes, for example, grow by condensation in Earth's atmosphere. In the solar nebula, dust grains were bombarded continuously by atoms of gas, and some of those stuck to the grains. A microscopic grain capturing a layer of gas molecules on its surface increases its mass by a much larger fraction than a gigantic boulder capturing a single layer of molecules. That is why condensation can increase the mass of a small grain rapidly, but, as the grain grows larger, condensation becomes less effective. The sequence of substances that condensed as the gas in the nebula cooled was described in the previous section.

The second process is accretion, the sticking together of solid particles. You may have seen accretion in action if you have walked through a snowstorm with big, Fluffy Flakes. If you caught one of those "flakes" on your glove and looked closely, you saw that it was made up of many tiny, individual flakes that had collided as they fell and accreted to form larger particles. In the solar nebula, the dust grains were, on average, no more than a few centimeters apart, so they collided frequently and could accrete into larger particles.

When the particles grew to sizes larger than a centimeter, they would have been subject to new processes that tended to concentrate them. One important effect was that the growing solid objects would have collected into the plane of the solar nebula. Small dust grains could not fall into the plane because the turbulent motions of the gas kept them stirred up, but larger objects had more mass, and gas motions could not have prevented them from settling into the plane of the spinning nebula. Astronomers calculate this would have concentrated the larger solid particles into a relatively thin layer about 0.01 AU thick hat would have made further growth more rapid. There is no clear distinction between a very large grain and a very small planetesimal, but you might consider an object to be a planetesimal when its diameter approaches a kilometer (0.6 mi) or so.

Through these processes, the theory proposes, the nebula became filled with trillions of solid particles ranging in size from pebbles to tiny planets. As the largest began to exceed 100 km in diameter, additional accretion processes began to affect them, and a new stage in planet building began, the formation of **protoplanets**, massive objects destined to become planets.

The Growth of Protoplanets

The coalescing of planetesimals eventually produced protoplanets. As these larger bodies grew, new processes altered their physical structure and helped them grow faster.

If planetesimals had collided at orbital velocities, it is unlikely they would have stuck together. A typical orbital velocity in the solar system is about 10 km/s (22,000 mph). Head-on collisions at this velocity would vaporize the material. However, the planetesimals were all moving in the same direction in the nebular plane and didn't collide head on. Instead, they merely "rubbed shoulders," so to speak, at low relative velocities. Such gentle collisions would have been more likely to combine planetesimals than to shatter them.

The largest planetesimals would grow the fastest because they had the strongest gravitational fi eld. Their stronger gravity could attract additional material, and they could also hold on to a cushioning layer to trap fragments. Astronomers calculate that the largest planetesimals would have grown quickly to protoplanetary dimensions, sweeping up more and more material.

The theory of protoplanet growth into planets supposes that all the planetesimals had about the same chemical composition. The planetesimals accumulated to form a planet-sized ball of material with homogeneous composition throughout. Once the planet formed, heat would begin to accumulate in its interior from the decay of short-lived radioactive elements.

The violent impacts of in-falling particles would also have released energy called heat of formation. These two heating sources would eventually have melted the planet and allowed it to differentiate. Differentiation is the separation of material according to density. Once a planet melted, the heavy metals such as iron and nickel, plus elements chemically attracted to them, would settle to the core, while the lighter silicates and related materials floated to the surface to form a low-density crust. The process of differentiation depends partly on the presence of short-lived radioactive elements whose rapid decay would have released enough heat to melt the interior of planets. Astronomers know such radioactive elements were present because the oldest meteorites contain daughter isotopes such as magnesium-26. That isotope is produced by the decay of aluminum-26 with a half-life of only 0.74 million years. The aluminum-26 and similar short-lived radioactive isotopes are gone now, but they must have been present during the earliest part of the solar system's history.

If planets formed by accretion of planetesimals and were later melted by radioactive decay and heat of formation, then Earth's early atmosphere may have consisted of a combination of gases delivered by planetesimal impacts and released from the planet's interior during differentiation. The creation of a planetary atmosphere from a planet's interior is called outgassing. Given the location of Earth in the solar nebula, gases released from its interior during differentiation would not have included as much water as Earth now has. So, some astronomers think that Earth's water and even some of its present atmosphere and biosphere accumulated late in the formation of the planet as Earth swept up volatile-rich planetesimals. These icy planetesimals would have formed in the cool outer parts of the solar nebula and could have been scattered toward the Terrestrial planets by encounters with the Jovian planets, creating a comet bombardment.

According to the solar nebula theory, the Jovian planets could begin growing by the same processes that built the Terrestrial planets. However, in the inner solar nebula, only metals and silicates could form solids, so the Terrestrial planets grew slowly. In contrast, the outer solar nebula contained not just solid bits of metals and silicates but also plentiful ices. Astronomers calculate that the Jovian planets would have grown faster than the Terrestrial planets and quickly become massive enough to begin even faster growth by a third planet-building process, **gravitational collapse**, drawing in large amounts of gas from the solar nebula.

The Jovian planets must have reached their present size in less than about 10 million years, before the sun become hot and luminous enough to blow away the remaining gas in the solar nebula, removing the raw material for further Jovian growth. As you will learn in the next section, disturbances from outside the forming solar system may have reduced the time available for Jovian planet formation even more severely. The Terrestrial planets, in comparison, grew from solids and not from the gas, so they could have continued to grow by accretion from solid debris left behind after the gas was removed. Mathematical models indicate that the Terrestrial planets were at least half finished within 10 million years but probably continued to grow for another 20 million years or so.

2
Kinds Of Planets

Planets of the solar system

The idea of what exactly <u>constitutes</u> a planet in the solar system has been traditionally the product of historical and cultural <u>consensus</u>. Ancient sky gazers applied the term *planet* to the seven celestial bodies that were observed to move appreciably against the background of the apparently fixed stars. These included the **Sun** and **Earth's <u>Moon</u>**, as well as the five planets in the modern sense—**Mercury, Venus, Mars, Jupiter,** and **Saturn**—that were readily visible as celestial wanderers before the invention of the telescope. After the idea of an Earth-centered cosmos was dispelled (*see* <u>Copernican system</u>) and more distinctions were made about the nature and movement of objects in the sky, the term *planet* was reserved only for those larger bodies that orbited the Sun. When the giant bodies Uranus and Neptune were discovered in 1781 and 1846, respectively, their obvious kinship with the other known planets left little question regarding their addition to the planetary ranks.

Of the eight currently recognized planets of the solar system, the inner four, from Mercury to <u>Mars</u>, are called <u>terrestrial planets</u>; those from Jupiter to Neptune are called <u>giant planets</u> or Jovian planets. Between these two main groups is a belt of numerous <u>small bodies</u> called <u>asteroids</u>. After Ceres and other larger asteroids were discovered in the early 19th century, the bodies in this class were also referred to as minor planets or planetoids, but the term *asteroid* is now used most widely.

Two Kinds of Planets - Terrestrial and Jovian Planets

1. The two kinds of planets are distinguished by their locations and masses. The four inner *Terrestrial planets* are quite different from the four outer

Jovian planet

2. Craters are common. Almost every solid surface in the solar system is covered with craters

3. The two groups of planets are also distinguished by properties such as the presence or absence of rings and the number of moons

DATA - *Terrestrial planets* and *Jovian planets*

1) The distinction between the Terrestrial planets and the Jovian planets is dramatic. The inner four planets, Mercury, Venus, Earth, and Mars, are Terrestrial planets, meaning they are small, dense, rocky worlds with little or no atmosphere. The outer four planets, Jupiter, Saturn, Uranus, and Neptune, are Jovian planets, meaning they are large, low-density worlds with thick atmospheres and liquid interiors.

1a) Of the Terrestrial planets, Earth is the most massive, but the Jovian planets are much more massive. Jupiter is over 300 Earth masses, and Saturn is nearly 100 Earth masses. Uranus and Neptune are 15 and 17 Earth masses.

2) Craters are common on all the surfaces in the solar system that are strong enough to retain them. Earth has about 150 impact craters, but many more have been erased by erosion. Besides the planets, the asteroids and nearly all the moons in the solar system are scarred by craters. Ranging from microscopic to hundreds of kilometers in diameter, these craters have been produced over the ages by meteorite impacts. When astronomers see a rocky or icy surface that contains few craters, they know that the surface is young

3) The Terrestrial planets have densities like that of rock or metal. The Jovian planets all have low densities, and Saturn's density is only 70 percent the density of water. It would float in a big-enough bathtub. The atmospheres of the Jovian planets are turbulent, and some are marked by great storms such as the Great Red Spot on Jupiter, but the atmospheres are not deep. If Jupiter were shrunk to a few centimeters in diameter, its atmosphere would be no deeper than the fuzz on a badly worn tennis ball

3a) The interiors of the Jovian planets contain small cores of heavy elements such as metals, surrounded by a liquid. Jupiter and Saturn contain hydrogen forced into a liquid state by high pressure. Less-massive Uranus and Neptune contain heavy-element cores surrounded by partially solid water mixed with heavy material such as rocks and minerals

The Terrestrial planets are drawn here to the same scale as the Jovian planets.

The Jovian planets have extensive systems of satellites. For example, Jupiter is orbited by four large moons discovered by Galileo in 1610, and dozens of smaller moons are discovered up to the present day.

3b) All four Jovian planets have ring systems. Saturn's rings are made of ice particles. The rings of Jupiter, Uranus, and Neptune are made of dark rocky particles. Terrestrial planets have no rings

Facts - *Terrestrial planets*

1. Planetary orbits to scale. The Terrestrial planets lie quite close to the sun, whereas the Jovian planets are spread far from the sun
2. Mercury is only 40 percent larger than Earth's moon, and its weak gravity cannot retain a permanent atmosphere. Like the moon, it is covered with craters from meteorite impacts
3. Mercury is so close to the sun that it is difficult to study from Earth. The Mariner 10 and MESSENGER spacecraft flew past Mercury in 1974 and 2008, respectively, and were able to take detailed close-up photos of the planet's surface.
4. The surface of Venus is not visible through its cloudy atmosphere, but radar maps reveal a dry desert world of craters and volcanoes.
5. Mars has a thin atmosphere and little water. Craters and volcanoes are common on its desert surface.

3

The Terrestrial Planets

Overview -

The Terrestrial worlds are made up of rock and metal. They are all differentiated, which means they are each separated into layers of different densities, with high-density materials on the inside and lower density materials on the outside.

when the planets formed, their surfaces were subjected to heavy bombardment by leftover planetesimals and debris in the young solar system. You will see lots of craters on these worlds, especially on Mercury and the moon, many of them dating back to the heavy bombardment era.

if a lava flow covered up some cratered landscape after the end of the heavy bombardment, few craters could be formed later on that surface because most of the debris in the solar system was gone. When you see a smooth plain on a planet, you can guess that surface is younger than the heavily cratered areas.

Atmospheres

Both Mercury and the moon's craters, plains, and mountains; they each have little or no atmosphere to obscure your view. In comparison, the surface of Venus is completely hidden by a cloudy atmosphere even thicker than Earth's. Mars, the medium-sized planet, has a relatively thin atmosphere.

Four Stages of Planetary Development

Differentiation- The first stage of planetary evolution is differentiation, the separation of material according to density. As you have already learned, Earth is differentiated: It has a dense metallic core, a less-dense rocky mantle, and a low-density crust. That differentiation is understood to have occurred due to melting of Earth's interior caused by heat from a combination of radioactive decay plus energy released by in-falling matter during the planet's formation. Once the interior of Earth melted, the densest materials were able to sink to the core

Cratering- The second stage, cratering, could not begin until a solid surface formed. The heavy bombardment of the early solar system made craters on Earth just as it did on the moon and other planets. As the debris in the young solar system cleared away, the rate of cratering impacts fell rapidly to its present low rate

Flooding- The third stage, flooding, began as radioactive decay continued to heat Earth's interior and caused rock to melt in the upper mantle, where the pressure was lower than in the deep interior. Some of that molten rock welled up through cracks in the crust and flooded the deeper impact basins. Later, as the environment cooled, water fell as rain and flooded the basins to form the first oceans.

slow surface evolution- The fourth stage, slow surface evolution, has continued for at least the past 3.5 billion years. Earth's surface is constantly changing as sections of crust slide over and against each other, push up mountains, and shift continents. In addition, moving air and water erode the surface and wear away geological features. Almost all traces of the first billion years of Earth's history have been destroyed by the active crust and erosion.

Earth – Our Home

It is geologically active, with a molten interior and heat flowing outward that powers volcanism, earthquakes, and moving crustal plates. Almost 75 percent of Earth's surface is covered by liquid water, unlike any other planet in our solar system, and the atmosphere contains a significant amount of oxygen, also unlike any other planet.

When the solar system formed, Earth was the largest predominantly solid object to take shape and acquired the most internal heat energy of the rocky planets. As a result, Earth was the most susceptible to the development of internal heat flows and to the breaking up of its surface into large slabs, or plates, which slowly grind past each other. Through a combination of plate movements known as plate tectonics, volcanic activity, and comet impacts, large amounts of water accumulated on Earth's surface. The planet's distance from the Sun, its gravity, and an insulating atmosphere combined to create conditions for this water to exist in each of its three physical states, including liquid water, which was essential to the development of life. As a result, Earth today appears unique, with its swirling water clouds, vast oceans, and continents colored green in parts by the presence of plants.

EARTH STRUCTURE

EARTH'S LAYERED INTERNAL STRUCTURE IS MIRRORED IN A MULTILAYERED ATMOSPHERE THAT EXTENDS FOR HUNDREDS OF MILES ABOVE THE PLANET'S SURFACE, GRADUALLY MERGING WITH SPACE.

What we know of Earth's internal structure has been learned largely through the study of earthquake waves, particularly the routes they take as they travel inside the planet. Each layer beneath the surface is progressively denser, hotter, and under increased pressure. A unique aspect of Earth is that its outer, rigid shell, the lithosphere (made up of the crust and topmost layer of the mantle), is split into chunks called tectonic plates, which move relative to each other, driven by internal heat flows. Surrounding the planet's surface, Earth's atmosphere provides important protection to the life that flourishes on the planet.

Earth Facts (Data) -

Earth layer by layer Earth has three primary layers—core, mantle, and crust—each with a unique chemical composition. The core has two distinct parts, inner and outer. There are also two types of crust—the thinner oceanic and the thicker continental crust. The layers of the mantle increase in density with depth, and the topmost layer is fused to the crust, forming the lithosphere.

Inner core The innermost layer of Earth consists of a solid iron–nickel alloy and has an average temperature of about 9,900°F (5,500°C). Despite the high temperature, the metals in the inner core cannot melt because of the intense pressure exerted on them.

Outer core

The outer core is liquid iron with some nickel and has an average temperature of about 9,000°F (5,000°C). Currents in the outer core are thought to generate Earth's magnetic field and cause the magnetic poles to wander.

Mantle

The largest of Earth's internal layers is basically solid, consisting of rocks such as peridotite. However, it can slowly deform, allowing heat to enter from the core and cause convection currents over geological time scales. These currents drive crustal movements.

Crust

Oceanic crust consists of dark volcanic rocks such as basalt and is 4–5 miles (7–8 km) thick. Continental crust consists of many types of relatively light rock and is 16–45 miles (25–70 km) thick.

Ocean Saltwater oceans cover almost three-quarters of Earth's surface and vary in depth up to 36,000 ft (11,000 m)

Atmosphere Earth's atmosphere consists mainly of nitrogen, oxygen, and argon, with small amounts of many other gases, including carbon dioxide. It has five layers, each defined by the way the temperature varies within its boundaries. In the troposphere and mesosphere, temperature falls with increasing height, while in the stratosphere and thermosphere, the temperature rises. The exosphere is so thin that the gas temperature there is of little significance.

The troposphere is the layer in which clouds form and weather occurs; it varies in thickness from about 10 miles (16 km) at the equator to 5 miles (8 km) at the poles.

The stratosphere is a relatively calm layer above the troposphere, about 19–25 miles (30–40 km) thick. Passenger aircraft fly in the bottom of the stratosphere, above the clouds.

The mesosphere is about 19–31 miles (30–50 km) thick; its upper boundary is the coldest part of the atmosphere at about –146°F (–100°C)

The thermosphere is a rarefied, ionized layer extending from about 53 miles (85 km) to 430 miles (700 km) above Earth's surface

The exosphere is the outermost, highly rarefied zone of Earth's atmosphere. Its outer edge forms a blue halo (corona) around Earth when viewed from space

TECTONIC EARTH

EARTH'S OUTER ROCKY SHELL IS SPLIT INTO MANY HUGE FRAGMENTS CALLED TECTONIC PLATES. THESE SLOWLY MOVING PLATES INTERACT, CAUSING VARIOUS GEOLOGICAL EVENTS AND CREATING CHANGES ON THE PLANET'S SURFACE. Earth's tectonic plates are irregularly shaped and fit together like a jigsaw puzzle. Their movements relative to each other, caused by convective heat flows deep within the planet, occur at a rate of just a few inches each year, but over millions of years, plate movement has shifted continents. A variety of features have formed at or near plate boundaries. These include mountain ranges, deep-sea trenches, volcanoes where two plates move toward each other, and mid-ocean ridges where they move apart. Earthquakes are more common at plate boundaries.

There are seven major plates—for example, the Pacific and Eurasian plates—as well as a dozen or so medium-sized plates, such as the Arabian Plate, and numerous much smaller microplates. Listed here are most of the recognized plates, in approximate order of decreasing size. The plates are also numbered on the globes shown on the right. A few of the microplates are sometimes considered just parts of larger plates.

North American

The North American Plate (2) makes up just under one-sixth of Earth's surface. It contains parts of the Arctic and Atlantic oceans and a section of Siberia. A notable volcanic hot spot has existed for millions of years under this plate and is currently the cause of vigorous geyser activity in Yellowstone National Park, Wyoming.

South American

With the neighboring Nazca (9), Scotia (18), and other smaller plates, the South American Plate (8) accounts for about one-eighth of Earth's surface. The Andes Mountain range in South America rises where the eastward-moving Nazca Plate is pushed under the edge of the South American Plate.

Eurasian

This plate (3) includes Europe and most of the landmass of Asia. Several medium-sized plates to the east and southeast, such as the Sunda Plate (11), were formerly considered part of the Eurasian Plate. Millions of years ago, the Indian Plate (10) crashed into the Eurasian Plate, creating the Himalayas.

African

The two African plates (4 and 5) include the African continent and large parts of the Atlantic and Indian oceans. Africa is believed to be in the process of splitting into two parts along the East African Rift—a gigantic split in Earth's crust that runs for about 2,500 miles (4,000 km) through East Africa.

Australian

This plate (7) comprises Australia, parts of New Zealand and New Guinea, and parts of the Indian and Southern oceans. Major features include Australia's deserts, the Great Dividing Range, and the Great Barrier Reef. The whole plate is moving in a northeastern direction at a rate of about 2.5 in (6.5 cm) per year.

Pacific

The largest tectonic plate, the Pacific Plate (1) covers about one-fifth of Earth. It contains no large landmasses, but many volcanic islands and subsea volcanoes occur where plumes of magma burst through the surface. The Pacific Plate is moving northwest at a rate of about 4 in (10 cm) per year.

Antarctic

Making up about one-eighth of Earth's surface, the Antarctic Plate (6) includes the Antarctic continent at its center, together with most of the encircling Southern Ocean. Over millions of years, this plate has become larger, as all around its edges new plate is continually created at divergent plate boundaries.

THE MOON

THE MOON, EARTH'S COMPANION IN SPACE, IS OUR PLANET'S LONE SATELLITE. IT IS THE LARGEST AND BRIGHTEST OBJECT IN THE NIGHT SKY AND THE ONLY ONE WHOSE SURFACE FEATURES CAN BE EASILY SEEN WITH THE NAKED EYE.

With a diameter one-quarter of Earth's, the Moon is the largest satellite in the solar system compared to its parent planet. Earth and the Moon exert a powerful influence on each other through their gravity. Tidal forces have slowed the Moon's rotation so that it spins once on its axis in the same time it takes to orbit Earth (27.32 days), and consequently keeps one face permanently toward our planet. The Moon is a barren ball of rock that lacks sufficient gravity to hold on to a substantial atmosphere. Exposed alternately to the heat of the Sun and the emptiness of space, the lunar surface experiences wild temperature swings, from 248°F (120°C) at local noon to –274°F (–170°C) in the middle of the long lunar night. The floors of permanently shadowed craters get even colder. With no weather or tectonic activity to erase craters, much of the Moon's battered landscape preserves a barely altered record of conditions in our part of the solar system over the last 4 billion years.

1.The Mare Serenitatis (Sea of Serenity) lies within an impact basin created 3.9 billion years ago. It is about 435 miles (700 km) in diameter.

2. The Montes Apenninus is the most prominent lunar mountain range, running southeast of the Imbrium Basin.

3.At 698 miles (1,123 km) across, the Mare Imbrium (Sea of Rains) is one of the largest lunar maria. It is ringed by mountains thrown up by the meteor strike that formed the Imbrium impact basin.

4. The Aristarchus Crater is a relatively young impact crater (450 million years old) and one of the Moon's brightest features.

5. The Clavius Crater is a huge ancient crater in the southern highlands. It is 140 miles (225 km) in diameter.

6. The well-defined Mare Crisium (Sea of Crises) fills an impact basin 345 miles (555 km) across.

7. The Mare Tranquillitatis (Sea of Tranquillity) was the site of the Apollo 11 Moon landing.

8. Eratosthenes Crater sits at the western end of Montes Apenninus. It is 36 miles (58 km) across and 2.2 miles (3.6 km) deep.

9. The Mare Nectaris (Sea of Nectar) is a small lunar mare that forms a "gulf" in the Sea of Tranquillity.

10. Tycho Crater measures 53 miles (86 km) across. It is surrounded by bright rays and dominates the southern highlands.

Northern hemisphere The Moon orbits bolt upright in relation to the Sun, so its polar regions receive horizontal sunlight. As a result, crater floors near the poles can be permanently shadowed and may contain water ice

Far side The hemisphere that faces away from Earth is more densely cratered than the near side. It has fewer of the dark lava plains, or maria, that dominate the near side, and those it does have are relatively small.

Southern hemisphere The south pole is located at the edge of a vast impact crater called the South Pole–Aitken Basin. Smaller craters within it contain areas of permanent shadow and ice from collisions with comets.

MOON STRUCTURE

AS A RELATIVELY SMALL BODY, THE MOON HAS COOLED CONSIDERABLY IN THE 4.5 BILLION YEARS SINCE ITS FORMATION. ITS ROCKY INTERIOR HAS LARGELY SOLIDIFIED AROUND A CORE OF RED-HOT OR PARTIALLY MOLTEN IRON. The Moon's proximity to Earth has permitted scientists to investigate its inner structure in detail. Using seismometers placed on the surface by astronauts during the Apollo Moon landings, geologists can map the lunar interior by measuring the properties of moonquakes—seismic tremors triggered when tidal forces distort the shape of the Moon, or when meteorite impacts send shock waves through its interior. More recently, spacecraft, including NASA's twin GRAIL (Gravity Recovery and Interior Laboratory) satellites, have mapped the Moon's structure by measuring slight variations in its gravitational field

The Moon's inner core is remarkably small, only around 150 miles (240 km) across

Birth of the Moon

Studies of lunar rock suggests that the Moon was formed around 4.5 billion years ago, when a Mars-sized world called Theia collided with the still-molten Earth. The impact obliterated Theia and blasted huge amounts of debris into orbit around Earth. Over time, much of this material came together to form a single large satellite—the Moon

Surface elevation

The Moon's highest regions are on its far side, which is on average 3 miles (5 km) higher than the near side. The lowest region—the 8-mile- (13-km-) deep South Pole–Aitken Basin—is also on the far side. Low-lying lava plains called maria (seas) cover 31 percent of the Moon's near side.

Lunar layers

The Moon has a layered internal structure with a thin crust and a very deep mantle, which is solid for most of its depth. In the Moon's center is an iron core heated to about 2,600°F (1,400°C) by energy from radioactive elements.

Crust The lunar crust probably originated as an ocean of molten magma. Made of granitelike silicate rock, the crust is about 30 miles (48km) thick on the near side and 46 miles (74km) thick on the far side.

Outer mantle The majority of the silica-rich lunar mantle is solid rock. It contains a higher proportion of iron than Earth's mantle. Earth's tidal forces have pulled the Moon's core about 1.2 miles (2 km) away from its exact center, slightly closer to the near side of the Moon.

Outer core This molten layer consists of liquid iron with small amounts of sulfur and nickel.

Inner core This is a ball of pure iron squeezed solid by the pressure of the rocks around it.

Inner mantle The lunar mantle is partially molten close to the Moon's core.

1. Lunar craters such as Euler, 27 km (17 mi) in diameter, look deep when you see them near the terminator where shadows are long, but a typical crater is only a fifth to a tenth as deep as its diameter, and large craters are even shallower. Because craters are formed by shock waves rushing outward, by the rebound of the rock, and by the expansion of hot vapors, craters are almost always round, even when the meteorite strikes at a steep angle.

1a). Rock ejected from distant impacts can fall back to the surface and form smaller craters called secondary craters. The chain of craters here is a 45-km-long chain of secondary craters produced by ejecta from the large crater Copernicus 200 km out of the frame to the lower right. Bright ejecta blankets and rays gradually darken as sunlight darkens minerals and small meteorites stir the dusty surface. Bright rays are signs of youth. Rays from the crater Tycho, perhaps only 100 million years old, Rock ejected from distant impacts can fall back to the surface and form smaller craters called secondary craters. The chain of craters here is a 45-km-long chain of secondary craters produced by ejecta from the large crater Copernicus 200 km out of the frame to the lower right. Bright ejecta blankets and rays gradually darken as sunlight darkens minerals and small meteorites stir the dusty surface. Bright rays are signs of youth. Rays from the crater Tycho, perhaps only 100 million years old, extend halfway around the moon.

1. Plum Crater, 40 m (130 ft) in diameter, was visited by Apollo 16 astronauts. Note the many smaller craters visible. Lunar craters range from giant impact basins to tiny pits in rocks struck by micrometeorites, meteorites of microscopic size.

2a). In larger craters, the deformation of the rock can form one or more inner rings concentric with the outer rim. The largest of these craters are called multiringed basins. In Mare Orientale on the west edge of the visible moon, the outermost ring is almost 900 km (550 mi) in diameter

2b). The energy of an impact can melt rock, some of which falls back into the crater and solidifies. When the moon was young, craters could also be flooded by lava welling up from below the crust. A few meteorites found on Earth have been identified chemically as fragments of the moon's surface blasted into space by cratering impacts. The fragmented nature of these meteorites indicates that the moon's surface has been battered by impact craters.

3. Most of the craters on the moon were produced long ago when the solar system was filled with debris from planet building. As that debris was swept up, the cratering rate fell rapidly, as shown below.

HIGHLANDS AND PLAIN

HE LUNAR LANDSCAPE CAN BE BROADLY DIVIDED INTO TWO DISTINCT TYPES OF TERRAIN: BRIGHT, HEAVILY CRATERED HIGHLANDS AND RELATIVELY SMOOTH, DARK PLAINS KNOWN AS LUNAR SEAS, OR MARIA.

The highlands represent the original ancient crust of the Moon, formed as its surface began to solidify from a molten magma ocean 4.5 billion years ago. They are dominated by bright silicate minerals similar to those of

Earth's crust, and they feature countless craters laid one on top of another over billions of years. The maria, meanwhile, are flat and sparsely cratered plains consisting of dark basaltic lavas. Studies of the boundaries between the two regions show that the lunar maria are later surfaces that have erased all traces of earlier craters.

Mercury

Mercury orbits so close to the sun that it is difficult to observe from Earth, and little was known about it until 1974–1975, when the Mariner 10 spacecraft flew past Mercury three times and revealed a planet whose surface is heavily cratered, much like that of Earth's moon. Analysis of the Mariner 10 data showed that large areas have been flooded by lava and then cratered. New information is arriving now from the MESSENGER spacecraft that will fly by Mercury three times during 2008–2010 and then settle into orbit around the planet in 2011. The largest impact feature on Mercury is the Caloris Basin, a ringed area that MESSENGER photos reveal as 1300 km (800 miles) in diameter, resembling the large ringed basin Mare Orientale ("Eastern Sea") on Earth's moon. The Caloris basin on Mercury and Mare Orientale on the moon both include concentric rings of cliffs formed by a large impact. Though Mercury looks moonlike, it does have several features that Earth's moon lacks. Mariner 10 photos revealed long curving ridges called lobate scarps up to 3 km (2 mi) high and 500 km (300 mi) long. The scarps even cut through craters, indicating that they formed after most of the heavy bombardment. The lobate scarps are the kind of faults that form by compression, but there are no faults on Mercury that could have formed by extension or stretching. This suggests that the entire crust was compressed long ago. MESSENGER photos revealed a "spider" of raised ridges appearing to extend from near a medium-sized crater; geologists are not sure what process could have caused the spider. Spectroscopic observations indicate that Mercury has an extremely thin atmosphere that may be partly outgassed from the crust and partly atoms captured from the solar wind. Mercury is quite dense, and models indicate that it must have a large metallic core . In fact, the metallic core occupies about 70 percent of the radius of the planet. In a sense, Mercury is a metal planet with a thin rock mantle and crust.

Venus

Venus to be much like Earth. Its diameter is 95 percent of Earth's , it has a similar average density and composition, and it is just 30 percent closer to the sun. The surface of Venus is perpetually hidden below thick clouds, and only in the past few decades have planetary scientists discovered that Venus is a deadly hot desert world of volcanoes, lava flows, and impact craters lying at the bottom of a deep ocean of hot gases.

The Atmosphere of Venus

In composition, the atmosphere of Venus is roughly **96** percent carbon dioxide. The rest is mostly nitrogen, with some argon, sulfur dioxide, and small amounts of sulfuric acid, hydrochloric acid, and hydrofluoric acid. There is only a tiny amount of water vapor. Overall, the composition is deadly unpleasant, and most certainly smells bad too. Spectra show that the impenetrable clouds that hide the surface are made up of droplets of sulfuric acid and microscopic crystals of sulfur.

This unbreathable atmosphere is 90 times denser than Earth's atmosphere. The air you breathe is **1000 times** less dense than water, but on Venus the air is only **10** times less dense than water. If you could survive the unpleasant conditions, you could strap wings on your arms and fly in Venus's atmosphere. The surface temperature on Venus is hot enough to melt lead, and you can understand that because the thick atmosphere creates a severe greenhouse effect. Sunlight filters down through the clouds and warms the surface, but heat cannot escape easily because the atmosphere is opaque to infrared radiation. Traces of sulfur dioxide and water vapor help trap the infrared, but it is the overwhelming abundance of carbon dioxide that makes the greenhouse effect on Venus much more severe than on Earth.

Weather on Venus

Venus is cloaked in clouds of sulfuric acid that block out 80 percent of all sunlight. The atmosphere glides rapidly around the planet on winds of up to 220 mph (360 km/h)—cloud systems can sail completely around the planet in under four days. Venus's clouds rain sulfuric acid, but the lower atmosphere is so hot that the raindrops evaporate before reaching the ground. The heavy cloud layer in Venus's atmosphere appears to shield it from most meteorite bombardments.

The Surface of Venus

Although the thick clouds on Venus are opaque to visible light, they are transparent to radio waves, so astronomers have been able to map Venus using radar. As early as 1965, Earth-based radio telescopes made low-resolution maps, but later both U.S. and Soviet spacecraft orbited Venus and mapped its surface by radar. Maps made in the early 1990s by the Magellan spacecraft reveal objects as small as 100 meters (300 ft) in diameter.

Radar maps of Venus are reproduced using arbitrary colors. In some maps, scientists have chosen to give Venus an overall orange glow because sunlight filtering down through the clouds bathes the landscape in a perpetual sunset glow. Other radar maps have been colored gray, the natural color of the rocks. In yet other maps, lowlands are colored blue, but there are no oceans on Venus. When you look carefully at colored radar maps of Venus, recall that its surface is a deadly dry desert.

By international agreement, names on Venus are all female, with three exceptions — Maxwell, a high mountain, and Alpha Regio and Beta Regio, two high volcanic peaks—which were all named before the international naming convention for Venus was adopted.

Radar maps show that Venus is similar to Earth in one way but strangely different in other ways. Nearly 75 percent of Earth's surface is covered by low-lying, basaltic seafloors, and 85 percent of Venus's surface is covered by basaltic lowlands. There is no liquid water on Venus, however, so its lowlands are not really seafloors, and the remaining highlands are not like the well defined continents you see on Earth.

The highland area Ishtar Terra, named for the Babylonian goddess of love, is about the size of Australia. At its eastern edge, the mountain called Maxwell Montes rises to an altitude of 12 km, with the impact crater Cleopatra on its lower slopes (for comparison, Mt. Everest, the tallest mountain on Earth, is 8.8 km high). Bounded by mountain ranges in the north and west, the center of Ishtar Terra is occupied by Lakshmi Planum, a great plateau about 4 km above the surrounding plains. The collapsed calderas Colette and Sacajawea suggest that Lakshmi Planum is a great lava plain. The mountains bounding Ishtar Terra, including Maxwell, resemble folded mountain ranges, which suggests that limited horizontal motion in the crust as well as volcanism may have helped form the highlands.

1 There are two main types of volcanoes found on Earth. Composite volcanoes are associated mostly with plate boundaries, and shield volcanoes are associated with hot spots that are not related to plate boundaries.

2 Volcanoes on Venus and Mars can be recognized by their shapes as being shield volcanoes, the kind produced by hotspot volcanism and not by plate tectonics.

3 Some volcanoes on Venus and Mars are very large. They have grown to great sizes because of repeated eruptions at the same place in the crust. This is also evidence that neither Venus nor Mars has been dominated by horizontal plate tectonics like Earth's.

VENUS STRUCTURE

Almost equal in size and density to Earth, Venus probably has much the same internal structure and chemistry. At the heart of the planet there is thought to be a metal core with a solid center and a molten outer layer. Surrounding this is a deep mantle of hot rock and a thin, brittle crust that shows abundant evidence of volcanic activity. Although Venus has a metal core like Earth's, it has no detectable magnetic field. This may be because it rotates too slowly—taking eight months to turn once—to produce the circulations within the outer core that would generate a dynamo effect. Venus has the thickest, most dense atmosphere of all the rocky planets. Its air is 96.5 percent carbon dioxide and contains small amounts of other chemicals, including sulfuric acid; a thick blanket of sulfuric acid clouds covers the entire planet.

Mantle

The mantle is hot, plastic rock, churned by convection currents that move slowly over thousands of years. Similar in composition to Earth's, Venus's mantle may contain rocks rich in iron and magnesium.

Crust

The thin outer layer above the mantle is made of basalt and other silicate rocks. In places the surface of the crust bulges outward, lifted by tremendous volcanic forces in the upper part of the mantle.

Venusian volcanoes

Venus does not have steep-sided, explosive volcanoes like typical volcanoes on Earth. Instead, most are shield volcanoes (shallow, gently sloping structures made from multiple layers of lava flows). On the lowland plains are types of volcanoes called pancake domes, formed by very thick lava, and tick volcanoes, with a central body and radiating leglike valleys. Other volcanic features include circular depressions called coronae and spiderlike arachnoids.

Volcanic hot spots Unlike Earth, Venus's surface is not broken into tectonic plates that create volcanoes as they move. Instead, Venusian volcanoes form above hot spots where plumes of hot magma well up from the interior. The result is runny lava that forms volcanoes of various sizes and shapes.

Maat Mons The second-highest mountain and the highest volcano on Venus, Maat Mons—named after the Egyptian goddess of truth and justice— rises nearly 3 miles (5 km) above the surrounding plains. It is a huge shield volcano with a caldera (crater) about 20 miles (30 km) across at the summit, and may be active.

Mead Crater

Most features on Venus are named after historical or mythological women. Mead Crater, for example, is named after cultural anthropologist Margaret Mead (1901–78) and is the largest impact crater on Venus, over 174 miles (280 km) across. It has two distinct, concentric rings. The bright inner ring is a cliff formed by the initial impact. The darker outer ring is crossed by streaks made by ejecta and probably formed when the whole structure later collapsed.

MARS

MARS IS A BITTERLY COLD DESERT WORLD, STAINED A RUSTY RED BY IRON-RICH DUST ON ITS SURFACE. THOUGH HALF THE DIAMETER OF EARTH AND MUCH FARTHER FROM THE SUN'S WARMTH, MARS SHOWS MANY STRIKING SIMILARITIES TO OUR HOME PLANET.

Northern hemisphere A permanent ice cap called the Planum Boreum (Northern Plain) sits on the north pole of Mars. Around 620 miles (1,000 km) across, its perimeter is formed from lobes of ice separated by deep, canyon-like troughs.

Eastern hemisphere Lava-covered plains dominate Mars's eastern face. The pale area in the lower left is Hellas Planitia, Mars's largest impact crater, at more than 1,243 miles (2,000km) wide. The dark zone to its north is Syrtis Major Planum, an expanse of dark, basaltic volcanic rock.

Southern hemisphere At Mars's south pole is the Planum Australe (Southern Plain), an ice cap with an upper layer of carbon-dioxide ice. Beyond it are huge areas of permafrost —water and soil frozen as hard as rock.

Western hemisphere This view of Mars is dominated by a vast canyon system called Valles Marineris. Wider than the Atlantic Ocean, it is probably a rift valley formed by ancient tectonic activity. Earth's Grand Canyon would fit inside one of its side channels

Regions -

1. Alba Mons is an enormous flat volcano surrounded by extensive lava fields
2. Tharsis region, a huge domed plateau about 2,485 miles (4,000 km) wide and home to giant volcanoes.
3. Olympus Mons is the largest volcano on Mars.
4. The southernmost of the three giant Tharsis volcanoes is Arsia Mons.

5. Acidalia Planitia is a large, flat lowland region.
6. The largest outflow channel on Mars, the Kasei Valles was formed by the sudden release of large volumes of water.
7. The Xanthe Terra region is the site of ancient river valleys and deltas.
8. Mutch Crater is a 124-mile- (199-km-) wide impact crater.
9. Hydraotes Chaos is a chaotic terrain with a jumble of different surface features, such as hills, mesas, valleys, and troughs.
10. Valles Marineris is an extensive network of deep canyons.
11. Dark regions are areas of relatively dust-free, bare volcanic rock.

The Atmosphere of Mars

The Martian air contains 95 percent carbon dioxide, 3 percent nitrogen, and 2 percent argon. That is much like the chemical composition of the air on Venus, but the Martian atmosphere is very thin, less than 1 percent as dense as Earth's atmosphere, one ten-thousandth as dense as Venus's atmosphere.

There is very little water in the Martian atmosphere, and the polar caps are composed of frozen water ice coated over by frozen carbon dioxide ("dry ice"). As summer comes to a Martian hemisphere, planetary scientists observe the carbon dioxide in that polar cap turning from solid to vapor and adding carbon dioxide to the atmosphere, while winter in the opposite hemisphere is freezing carbon dioxide out of the atmosphere and adding it to that polar cap.

Liquid water cannot survive on the surface of Mars because the air pressure is too low. Any liquid water would immediately boil away; and if you stepped out of a spaceship on Mars without your spacesuit, your body heat would make your blood boil. Whatever water is present on Mars must be frozen in the polar caps or in the form of **permafrost** within the soil.

Although the present atmosphere of Mars is very thin, you will see evidence that the climate once permitted liquid water to flow over the surface, so Mars must have once had a thicker atmosphere. As a Terrestrial planet, it should have outgassed significant amounts of carbon dioxide, nitrogen, and water vapor; but because it was small, it could not hold onto its gases. The escape velocity on Mars is only 5 km/s, less than half of Earth's, so it was easier for rapidly moving gas molecules to escape into space.

Mars has no ozone layer to protect its atmosphere from ultraviolet radiation. The ultraviolet photons can break atmospheric molecules up into smaller fragments, which escape more easily. Water, for example, can be broken up into hydrogen and oxygen. Thus, Mars is large enough to have had a substantial atmosphere when it was young, and may have had water falling as rain and collecting in rivers and lakes. It gradually lost much of its atmosphere and is now a cold, dry world.

Surface of Mars

Spacecraft have been visiting Mars for almost 40 years, but the pace has picked up recently. A small fleet of spacecraft has gone into orbit around Mars to photograph and analyze its surface, and five spacecraft have landed. Two Viking landers touched down in 1976, and three rovers have landed in recent years. Pathfinder and its rover Sojourner landed in 1997. Rovers Spirit and Opportunity landed in January 2004 and carried sophisticated instruments to explore the rocky surface, The Phoenix robot laboratory landed in the north polar region in 2008.

Data recorded by orbiting satellites show that the southern hemisphere of Mars is a heavily cratered highland region estimated to be at least 2 to 3 billion years old. The northern hemisphere is mostly a much younger lowland plain with few craters. This lowland plain may have been smoothed by lava flows, but growing evidence suggests that it was once filled with an ocean, a controversial hypothesis discussed in the next section.

Volcanism on Mars is dramatically evident in the Tharsis region, a highland region of volcanoes and lava flows bulging 10 km (6 mi) above the surrounding surface. A similar uplifted volcanic plain, the Elysium region, is more heavily cratered and eroded and appears to be older than the Tharsis bulge. The lack of many impact craters suggests that some volcanoes have been active within the last few hundred million years. There is no reason to think the volcanoes are completely dead.

All of the volcanoes on Mars are shield volcanoes, which are produced by hot spots penetrating upward through the crust. Shield volcanoes are not related to plate tectonics and are not evidence of plate motion on Mars. In fact, the largest volcano on Mars, Olympus Mons, provides clear evidence that plate tectonics has not been significant on Mars. Olympus Mons is 600 km (370 mi) in diameter at its base and rises 21 km (13 mi) high. The largest volcano on Earth is Mauna Loa in Hawaii, rising only 10 km (6 mi) above its base on the seafloor. Mauna Loa is so heavy that it has sunk into Earth's crust, producing an undersea moat around its base. In contrast, Olympus Mons, two times higher, has no moat and is supported entirely by the Martian crust. Evidently, the crust of Mars is much stronger than Earth's.

Water on Mars

MARS IS A DRY WORLD. IT HAS WATER ABOVE, ON, AND UNDER ITS SURFACE, BUT THE WATER IS IN THE FORM OF VAPOR OR ICE. LIQUID WATER WAS ONCE ABUNDANT ON MARS, AND ITS EFFECT ON THE LANDSCAPE IS STILL EVIDENT.

Today, liquid water cannot exist on the Martian surface because of the low temperature and atmospheric pressure. However, sedimentary rocks built up by water-deposited material, minerals formed by standing water, and landscape features shaped by flowing water all point to the fact that Mars may once have had large volumes of liquid water.

Water in Past

Billions of years ago, when Mars was a warmer planet, riverbeds and channel-like valleys hundreds of miles long formed as fast-flowing water carved through the landscape, and catastrophic floods covered vast areas, leaving floodplains behind. Valleys such as Kasei Valles, the site of two giant waterfalls eight times the height of Earth's Niagara Falls, are now dry. So too are Mars's deltas, lakes, and shallow seas. Increasing our knowledge of the planet's watery past helps in our search for life. Liquid water is essential for life— if it once existed on Mars, then perhaps life did too.

Evidence in rocks These gray balls, each about 0.2 in (4 mm) wide, lie scattered over a rocky outcrop in Eagle Crater. Analysis by the Opportunity rover in 2004 showed the balls consist of an iron mineral called hematite. Originally embedded in the outcrop, they collect on the ground after the softer rock erodes away. On Earth, hematite typically forms in lakes, so the same could have occurred on Mars. The circular patch is where Opportunity analyzed the underlying rock for comparison.

This plot shows the ability of planets to retain atmospheres. Dots represent the escape velocity and temperature of various solar system bodies. The lines represent the typical highest velocities of gas molecules of various masses. The Jovian planets have high escape velocities and can hold on to even the lowest mass molecules. Mars can hold only the more massive molecules, and the moon has such a low escape velocity that all gas molecules can escape.

Water today Most of the water on Mars today is locked within its frozen ice caps or held as vapor in its atmosphere. Orbiting spacecraft have also detected ice below the surface in other locations. Recently formed gullies on crater walls could be evidence of liquid groundwater released onto the surface.

Water ice This huge sheet of water ice is a permanent feature in an unnamed crater near the Martian north pole. The ice is 9 miles (15 km) across and sits on a field of sand dunes. Water ice is also visible on parts of the crater's rim and wall.

Clouds on Mars Four Mars Global Surveyor images show the progression of water-ice clouds (in blue) across the planet. These occasional, wispy, cirrus-type clouds occur when atmospheric water vapor forms ice crystals. Water vapor can also form a low-lying mist and early morning frost

Ice under the surface The Phoenix Mars Lander was the first craft to explore Mars's arctic region on the ground. In 2008, it landed near the northern polar cap. Using its robotic arm, it dug into the ground, exposing ice just inches below the surface. Four days later, the ice had vaporized.

Gullies Root-shaped gullies on the walls of impact craters may indicate that water still flows. Observations show that the gullies change with the seasons. Mars is too cold for pure water to be liquid, but briny groundwater, which has a lower freezing point, may be released to briefly carry fine-grained sediment down the walls.